Thoughts of Impact

by

Darrius Geter

21 Thoughts to Impact Your Life

Devotional

Impactful Publishing

SNELLVILLE, GA

Copyright © 2021 Darrius Geter

Cover Design by ProGraphic 260
Cover Photo by H.D. II Images
Cover Copyright © 2021 by Impactful Publishing, LLC.

All rights reserved. No part of this book may be reproduced in any form or by any electronic or mechanical means, including scanning, uploading, downloading, storage, and retrieval systems, without permission in writing from the publisher, except by a reviewer who may quote brief passages in review.

Unless otherwise indicated, Scriptures are taken from the English Standard Version. Copyright © 2001 by Crossway.

Scripture quotations noted as NKJV are taken from the New King James Version. Copyright © 2012 by Tyndale House Publishers, Inc. Wheaton, Illinois 60189. All rights reserved.

Scripture quotations noted as KJV are taken from the Holy Bible: King James Version.

Scripture quotations noted as NIV are taken from the New International Version © 1973, 1978, 1984, 2011 by Zondervan.

Scripture quotations noted as AMP are taken from the Amplified Bible © 2001 by the Lockman Foundation.

Printed in the United States of America

Impactful Publishing, LLC.
P.O. Box 1322

Snellville, Georgia 30078

The Impactful Publishing name and logo are trademarks of Impactful Publishing, LLC.

The publisher is not responsible for websites (or their content) that the publisher does not own.

Print ISBN: 978-0-578-90531-0
eBook ISBN: 978-0-578-90532-7

DEDICATION

To my beautiful wife Dayvener, who always believes in me, motivates me, and encourages me to push forward.

Your tomorrow is established by what you speak today. Begin establishing your future by speaking over it today! God did not create us to adapt to our situations; He created us to conquer them.

Table of Contents

Day One	Being Thankful	9
Day Two	Trust in the Lord	13
Day Three	Getting Out of Your Comfort Zone	17
Day Four	Moving Mountains	21
Day Five	Walking by Faith	25
Day Six	Having a Proper Attitude	29
Day Seven	Courage	33
Day Eight	Forgiveness	37
Day Nine	Decree a Thing	41
Day Ten	Refreshing Your Relationship with God	45
Day Eleven	Having Purpose	51
Day Twelve	Exercising Your Faith Part 1	55
Day Thirteen	Exercising Your Faith Part 2	61
Day Fourteen	Exercising Your Faith Part 3	67
Day Fifteen	Exercising Your Faith Part 4	73
Day Sixteen	Stretched to the Next Level Part 1	79
Day Seventeen	Stretched to the Next Level Part 2	83
Day Eighteen	Stretched to the Next Level Part 3	89
Day Nineteen	Stretched to the Next Level Part 4	93
Day Twenty	Spiritual Fullness	97
Day Twenty-One	Pursuing Your Destiny	101
About the Author		115

Day One

BEING THANKFUL

"By him, therefore, let us offer the sacrifice of praise to God continually, that is, the fruit of our lips giving thanks to his name."

- Hebrews 13:15 KJV

There is no question that we love God; if we did not, we would not make the effort to seek after His face. Although we love God, we must make sure we never take Him or His goodness in our life for granted.

So often in our life, we forget to fill God's ears with our heartfelt thanks. Sure, we thank Him for our food and for watching over us daily, but we have focused so much on surface-level issues that our prayers have become routine and lack the passion of being heartfelt and sincere.

We also tend to focus more on the things that are *missing* from our lives rather than all the good we have *flowing* in our lives. Sure, we would all like to have an extra million dollars in the bank but let us thank God that we had enough to pay our bills even if we are left with are a few dollars afterward.

We must take the time in our prayers to think deeply about the things that *are* going on in our life rather than what is *not* going on in our life and flood the gates of Heaven with our thanks. We must thank God for the peace we have in our life. We never realize how valuable peace is until we no longer have it.

We need to thank God for the things that did not go the way that we wanted it to go. He sees further than us and we should recognize that sometimes He may be shielding us from having to go through tumultuous situations that would have arisen had we gotten our way.

We often see the ungratefulness that others show us, but we seldom see the ungratefulness we show God. God loves us more than we can ever imagine and there is nothing we can do to earn or even repay Him for the love He has for us. Each day we should lift our voices and fill His temple with praise and thanksgiving.

THOUGHTS OF IMPACT

Thought of Impact:

As we spend time in prayer, the first thing we should do is thank God for how good He is. If we must choose between asking God for something or thanking Him for what He's done already, let us choose thanksgiving.

When we show that we are truly thankful and grateful for how God displays His love in our lives, He will begin to pour more of His blessings into our lives.

21 Thoughts to Impact Your Life

Your Thoughts:

_____

_____

_____

_____

_____

_____

_____

_____

_____

_____

"By him, therefore, let us offer the sacrifice of praise to God continually, that is, the fruit of our lips giving thanks to his name."
- Hebrews 13:15 KJV

THOUGHTS OF IMPACT

Your Thoughts:

_____

_____

_____

_____

_____

_____

_____

_____

_____

"By him, therefore, let us offer the sacrifice of praise to God continually, that is, the fruit of our lips giving thanks to his name."
- Hebrews 13:15 KJV

TRUST IN THE LORD

"Trust in the Lord with all your heart, and do not lean on your own understanding"
- *Proverbs 3:5*

When we look at the situations that are going on in our life, we cannot help but look at them from a natural perspective. Meaning we cannot help but look at them and analyze what the probable outcome is going to be based upon our own intellect, worldly experiences, and personal understanding.

However, we are urged here in this Proverb to *"lean not on our own understanding."* When we lean on our own understanding, we block God from moving in our lives because we have limited our expectations of what He can do in our situation to a natural framework that prohibits God from doing the supernatural.

We must expand our expectations within our situations that allow us to view them from a perspective that says; although according to worldly standards the outcome can be predicted, we believe that with our God, anything is possible! When we believe anything is possible in our life, we open our spirits for God to work miracles in our lives.

We must begin to understand the essence of faith. Faith is believing what God's Word says for my life is what's going to happen in my life. However, we do not always know exactly how God will bring His promises to fruition in our lives, so we must; *"lean not on our own understanding,"* but do what the Proverb writer says in verse 6.

In verse 6, the writer says, *"In all your ways acknowledge Him, and He will direct your paths"* (Proverbs 3:6 ESV). In everything we do, we are to first pray and seek direction from God and allow Him to direct our path. As God directs our path, we must faithfully follow where He is leading.

God might tell us to go left, but our own understanding might tell us that going left will lead us to a dead end. Since we are not leaning to our own understanding but allowing God to direct our path, we have just stepped out of the natural realm of operating where our possibilities are limited and into the supernatural realm of operating where our possibilities are limitless.

Thought of Impact:

As you go about your day, don't limit what God can do in your life by confining Him to only move according to your understanding. Allow God to have free reign in your life by going in the unexpected directions He's trying to lead you into.

Remember, faith is knowing what the finished outcome is supposed to be but not necessarily knowing the route, we must take to get there.

21 Thoughts to Impact Your Life

Your Thoughts:

_____

_____

_____

_____

_____

_____

_____

_____

_____

"Trust in the Lord with all your heart, and do not lean on your own understanding"
Proverbs 3:5

THOUGHTS OF IMPACT

Your Thoughts:

_____

_____

_____

_____

_____

_____

_____

_____

_____

"Trust in the Lord with all your heart, and do not lean on your own understanding"
Proverbs 3:5

Day Three

GETTING OUT OF YOUR COMFORT ZONE

"Peter answered Him. 'Lord, if it is you, command me to come to you on the water.'"
- *Matthew 14:28*

So often, when we venture out of our comfort zone into new and unfamiliar territory, we tend to feel more apprehensive than usual. The reason for this uneasy feeling is we are focusing on our own abilities and looking at what we can and cannot do from our limited perspective. What we should do is keep our eyes on Jesus because through Him, we can do all things.

When the disciples saw Jesus walking on water, only one (Peter); took it as an opportunity to step out of his comfort zone into the unknown. Once Peter took his eyes off Jesus and looked at the water, the wind, and the raging waves, he knew he did not have the ability to walk on water.

Once he began to look at his situation in contrast to his natural ability, he started to sink into the water. Peter began to doubt the possibility of being successful in what he was doing, which was walking on water.

We can do all things when we focus on Jesus and His abilities rather than our abilities. When we step out of our comfort zone and keep our eyes on Jesus instead of ourselves, we will experience things we have never experienced before and do things we never thought possible.

When we step out of our comfort zone with our eyes stayed on Jesus rather than on ourselves, a whole new world will be opened to us.

Thought of Impact:

As you go into the world, new opportunities and experiences may be made available to you. When these opportunities arise, focus on what God wants you to do outside your comfort zone by focusing on Him rather than denying new opportunities and possibilities because you are focusing on yourself and your own abilities.

Your Thoughts:

_____

_____

_____

_____

_____

_____

_____

_____

_____

_____

"Peter answered Him. 'Lord, if it is you, command me to come to you on the water.'"
Matthew 14:28

THOUGHTS OF IMPACT
Your Thoughts:

_____

_____

_____

_____

_____

_____

_____

_____

_____

"Peter answered Him. 'Lord, if it is you, command me to come to you on the water.'"
Matthew 14:28

Day Four

MOVING MOUNTAINS

"Jesus answered them, Truly, I say to you, if you have faith and do not doubt, you will not only do what has been done to the fig tree but even if you say to this mountain, 'Be taken up and thrown into the sea,' it will happen."

- Matthew 21:21

Looking back over the events that proceeded Jesus' statements, Jesus had just cursed the fig tree and watched it immediately shrivel up and die. Amazed by this, the disciples began to ask Jesus how it was possible for the fig tree to wither at His commands. Jesus' reply is simply that if you have faith, you will have whatever you ask for regardless of how big or how impossible it seems.

When we look at many of the issues we face in our lives, we often become overwhelmed by them because the sheer magnitude of how big the problems are and what we need to overcome the problem seems impossible to receive.

When we live our lives in frustration over how big our problems are and feel hopeless of ever overcoming them, we allow ourselves to be placed in bondage.

To be in bondage means that we are bound by and subjected to external power and are under its control. Because we are under the control of the problem that is overwhelming us, we have become a slave to it. And all our efforts in that area of our lives revolve around trying to appease the problem as we make fruitless efforts trying to get out of the mess we find ourselves.

However, Jesus is telling us that we do not have to live like that. Jesus said if we have faith and do not doubt, we can move mountains. So, I ask you today what mountains are you facing in your life?

How long have you had to stare at those mountains? Wouldn't it be nice to wake up in the morning and have a fresh view of different scenery rather than the same old issues you have been waking up to for the past few years or maybe even longer staring you back in the face?

I encourage you today to start speaking to your mountains and make a declaration in the name of Jesus that those mountains must be cast aside. Say mountain; you have enslaved me for far too long, you have made me live in fear for far too long, you have hindered my progress and my plans for far too long, you have dictated to me how I will live my life for far too long.

Right now, in the name of Jesus, I declare that you must be moved! I declare that my scenery is going to change!

Address your mountain by name so that your mountain knows you are talking to it.

Marriage; you must get right! Finances, you must get right! Health you must get right! Debt; I curse you at the root and declare that you must die in my life! Sickness, I curse you at the root and declare that you must die in my life!

Whatever your issue, start speaking to it in faith and not doubt. Expect to see changes manifesting in your life and keep speaking the Word of God to your mountains until you see what you are speaking fully come to fruition. Let us put faith to work in our lives and begin casting our mountains into the sea.

Thought of Impact:

If we have doubt which is the opposite of God's promises, we will continue to see the same old mountains controlling our life today, tomorrow, and forever. The key to us moving the mountains in our lives rests in our faith which is the promises of God. Either we have faith in God's Word, or we have doubt; there is no in-between.

21 Thoughts to Impact Your Life

Your Thoughts:

_____

_____

_____

_____

_____

_____

_____

_____

_____

_____

"Jesus answered them, Truly, I say to you, if you have faith and do not doubt, you will not only do what has been done to the fig tree but even if you say to this mountain, 'Be taken up and thrown into the sea,' it will happen."
- Matthew 21:21

THOUGHTS OF IMPACT
Your Thoughts:

_____

_____

_____

_____

_____

_____

_____

_____

_____

_____

_____

"Jesus answered them, Truly, I say to you, if you have faith and do not doubt, you will not only do what has been done to the fig tree but even if you say to this mountain, 'Be taken up and thrown into the sea,' it will happen."
- *Matthew 21:21*

Day Five

WALKING BY FAITH

"For we walk by faith, not by sight."

- *2 Corinthians 5:7*

As Christians, we can never hear enough about how important it is to walk by faith. Walking by faith means we live our lives trusting and believing the promises of God. When we live our lives according to faith, we live our lives acknowledging what the outcome is going to be and not the road we must take to get there.

However, if we live our lives according to what we see going on around us, we place ourselves in danger of not reaching the established outcome God intended for our lives.

When we live our lives according to what we see, we begin to determine what the outcome of our situation will be based on what is going on around us rather than what God has promised us.

When we look at God's promises for our lives, we can look at the situations we are facing and see the outcome that God has for us. However, we must not be swayed or moved from believing what God has promised us even when everything in our lives is going contrary to fulfilling that promise.

This is why it is important for us to be submitted to the leadership of the Holy Spirit so that the Fruit of the Spirit, especially patience, can manifest in our lives. When everything around us is saying that God's promise does not look like it is going to be fulfilled and even when our own fleshly emotions begin to make us feel like we are not going to have the outcome we need for our lives, we must place it all under the submission of our spirit which is led by the Holy Spirit. We must maintain an overall state of patience, allowing the full manifestation of God's promises to happen in our lives without us aborting the process by being consumed with doubt.

Thought of Impact:

THOUGHTS OF IMPACT

Since we live our life by faith, trusting and believing in the promises of God, we will not be moved by what we see. We must continue to speak the promises of God over our lives and maintain patience until God brings around the full manifestation of what He promised us.

21 Thoughts to Impact Your Life

Your Thoughts:

_____

_____

_____

_____

_____

_____

_____

_____

_____

"For we walk by faith, not by sight."
- *2 Corinthians 5:7*

THOUGHTS OF IMPACT

Your Thoughts:

_____

_____

_____

_____

_____

_____

_____

_____

_____

"For we walk by faith, not by sight."
- 2 Corinthians 5:7

Day Six

HAVING A PROPER ATTITUDE

"Do all things without complaining and disputing, that you may become blameless and harmless, children of God without fault in the midst of a crooked and perverse generation, among whom you shine as lights in the world."

- Philippians 2:14-15 NKJV

Our Attitude determines whether we will be successful or fail before we do anything in our life. Having the proper attitude and outlook for your life is essential to experiencing the goodness of life.

Our Attitude is a direct reflection of the quality of effort we are going to put into something. Our attitude reflects how we are going to face and deal with the obstacles that arise in our life.

The scripture tells us that we are to *"do all things without grumbling and faultfinding and complaining."* In a nutshell, the scripture is tells us whatever we engage in should be done with a positive attitude to ensure that our mindset has established the expectation of success.

We all tend to complain. We complain when things are not going our way, we complain when things do go our way, expressing how they could have been better. We tend to find fault with everything and everyone other than ourselves.

When we complain, what we are doing is declaring that the ways of God are not satisfactory to us. When we complain, we are saying God does not know how to effectively or appropriately do what He is doing in our lives.

Since complaining changes our mind from thinking positively to thinking negatively, we walk expecting failure because we do not believe our situation is set up for us to walk in victory.

In all things, we are to do everything with a positive attitude. We are to walk expecting victory. We must walk knowing that no matter what obstacles we face, no matter what confines us, we know that we are assured victory because of the God we serve.

We should live each day with a positive attitude. We should expect good things to happen, we should expect the very best that life has to offer; we should look for the good and look for unexpected opportunities in whatever situation we find ourselves. When we live our lives and face our day with a positive attitude, half the battle is already won.

As we approach the day with a positive attitude, we stand ready to face any problem, circumstance, and situation, knowing we will be victorious.

Thought of Impact:

I encourage you today to check your attitude daily. Check your attitude about your job, your relationships, your finances, even your relationship and with God. If you engage any area of your life with a negative attitude, you can only expect negative results.

21 Thoughts to Impact Your Life

Your Thoughts:

_____

_____

_____

_____

_____

_____

_____

_____

_____

"Do all things without complaining and disputing, that you may become blameless and harmless, children of God without fault in the midst of a crooked and perverse generation, among whom you shine as lights in the world."
- *Philippians 2:14-15 NKJV*

THOUGHTS OF IMPACT

Your Thoughts:

_____

_____

_____

_____

_____

_____

_____

_____

_____

_____

_____

"Do all things without complaining and disputing, that you may become blameless and harmless, children of God without fault in the midst of a crooked and perverse generation, among whom you shine as lights in the world."
- *Philippians 2:14-15 NKJV*

Day Seven

COURAGE

"No man shall be able to stand before you all the days of your life. Just as I was with Moses, so I will be with you. I will not leave you or forsake you. Be strong and courageous, for you shall cause this people to inherit the land that I swore to their fathers to give them."

- *Joshua 1:5-6*

In the scripture, Joshua has just been informed by God that Moses His servant is dead and Joshua is now appointed by God as Israel's new leader. God tells Joshua to be strong and courageous because He will not leave him nor forsake him.

This was probably a very intimidating time for Joshua as he has now been charged to march Israel into battle to begin taking the Promised Land that God had given to them as an inheritance. It's possible Joshua felt a little apprehensive about stepping into the leadership role over Israel and intimidated by the assignment given to him by God; it did not show because he lived his life and fulfilled his purpose with courage.

If there is anything we should carry with us daily, it is courage. Being courageous enables us to face difficulty, danger, or pain despite our fears.

Fear paralyzes us and makes it difficult for us to advance towards victory. Fear makes it difficult for us to face the problems in our lives and avoid dealing with the challenging situations that hold us back.

One of the main reasons people are not willing to deal with the problems they have in life is because they lack courage. One of the main reasons people are afraid to face each new day with joy and happiness is because they lack courage.

Courage is essential for us to face every new day God gives us. We don't have to do anything great or grand to obtain courage, but we can be assured that we already have courage flowing in our lives because we have God. Just as God told Joshua; we too can be assured that He will never leave us nor forsake us.

We must live our lives courageously because we are not only striving to possess the promises God has for us, but we are laying the foundation for our bloodline. God told Joshua to be courageous because he was being charged with taking control of the land promised to their ancestors and establishing a new nation.

Just as Joshua led Israel to seize what was promised to their forefathers, there are things that God desires for your children and your grandchildren to possess. Still it begins with us being courageous enough to follow the Spirit of God to lay a foundation for them to build on.

God told Joshua to continue to follow the law and do not turn to the right or the left, and he would continuously prosper. Although we no longer live according to the Law, if we follow God and do not deviate from Him, success will follow us everywhere we go.

Thought of Impact:

Our courage comes from our trust in God, not trust in ourselves. Let us continue to place our trust in God and His promises because if we do, we will live a life filled with courage.

21 Thoughts to Impact Your Life

Your Thoughts:

"No man shall be able to stand before you all the days of your life. Just as I was with Moses, so I will be with you. I will not leave you or forsake you. Be strong and courageous, for you shall cause this people to inherit the land that I swore to their fathers to give them."

- *Joshua 1:5-6*

THOUGHTS OF IMPACT

Your Thoughts:

_____

_____

_____

_____

_____

_____

_____

_____

_____

"No man shall be able to stand before you all the days of your life. Just as I was with Moses, so I will be with you. I will not leave you or forsake you. Be strong and courageous, for you shall cause this people to inherit the land that I swore to their fathers to give them."

- Joshua 1:5-6

Day Eight

FORGIVENESS

"For if you forgive others their trespasses, your heavenly Father will also forgive you, but if you do not forgive others their trespasses, neither will your Father forgive your trespasses."

- *Matthew 6:14-15*

In our life, there are some people who have undoubtedly done us wrong. There are also people in our life right now that are not living up to our standards, and because of that, we have animosity towards them.

When we live our life with unforgiveness and hatred towards others, it does very little to hurt them, but it poisons our very spirit. Unforgiveness and animosity make it difficult for us to trust others. It makes it difficult for us to move on from the hurt we are experiencing in life. It makes us live a life of regret as we wish we never made the mistake of inviting certain people into our lives.

Animosity towards others causes us to blame them for the negative things happening in our lives. We continuously think or say, if you would have done this or if you would not have done that, then I would not be in my current situation.

We must not blame others for our life situations, knowing that in many cases, the people closest to us did not and do not mean to cause us any harm. But we must not be naïve enough to think that no one ever intends to wrong us.

However, whether they intend to do us wrong or unintentionally bring us harm by not living up to our standards and doing the things we desire for them not to do in our lives, we must inevitably forgive them.

We must understand that as good of a life as we have tried to live, we too have done wrong. We have wronged others, and we have wronged our Heavenly Father by not living up to His standards. Despite it all, God has and continues to forgive us for all our wrongs. Because He forgives us of sins that require an eternal punishment, He expects us to forgive those in our life whose actions only cause short-term pain and disappointment.

Thought of Impact:

Think to yourself about the people in your life that have or are currently doing you wrong. Think about the people you have animosity towards because they are not living up to your standards.

As you think about these people and the situations that caused your pain and anger towards them, ask God to give you the strength and the power to forgive them. Once you release them from the anger generated by your unforgiveness towards them, God can begin to heal the hurt in your life and help you to move forward.

Your Thoughts:

_____

_____

_____

_____

_____

_____

_____

_____

_____

_____

"For if you forgive others their trespasses, your heavenly Father will also forgive you, but if you do not forgive others their trespasses, neither will your Father forgive your trespasses."
- *Matthew 6:14-15*

THOUGHTS OF IMPACT

Your Thoughts:

_____

_____

_____

_____

_____

_____

_____

_____

_____

"For if you forgive others their trespasses, your heavenly Father will also forgive you, but if you do not forgive others their trespasses, neither will your Father forgive your trespasses."
- *Matthew 6:14-15*

21 Thoughts to Impact Your Life

DECREE A THING

"Thou shalt also decree a thing, and it shall be established unto thee: and the light shall shine upon thy ways."

- Job 22:28

As Christians, we have gotten into the habit of taking whatever life throws at us. We wake up each day and go out into the world not knowing what to expect. We allow our life to simply unfold as it sees fit.

We have forgotten the fact that we were created in the image of God. God has given us dominion over everything on Earth. That means we walk in authority. *Authority* is the *power* or *right* to do something, particularly giving orders and seeing that they are carried out. To walk in authority means we have a right to dictate and determine the situations and circumstances of our life.

God told Job, *"if you lay your gold in the dust and consider it to be of little worth to you and make me the Almighty your gold and the Lord your precious silver, you shall decree a thing and it shall be established for you; and the light of God's favor will shine upon your ways."*

God is telling Job; if you take everything in your life that the world considers being of value and place Me above it all, I will grant you the right to not only *decree a thing in your life* but I will commit my favor upon all that you do so that you may consistently prosper and advance in your life.

As we go about our daily lives, let us make nothing and no one more valuable than the God we serve. Let us treat our God like a rare and precious treasure. For honoring God in such high esteem, God will grant us the ability to decree a thing, and it shall come to pass.

Since God has given us the right to decree a thing and has committed to allowing His favor to shine upon all our ways, we should not allow our life to unfold as it pleases, but our today should be a reflection of the thing we decreed yesterday.

Thought of Impact:

As you go about your day, begin identifying the areas of your life that need to change. Begin declaring and decreeing changes over those situations and circumstances in your life so that your tomorrow will be what you decide today and not what life chooses to throw at you.

21 Thoughts to Impact Your Life

Your Thoughts:

_____

_____

_____

_____

_____

_____

_____

_____

_____

"Thou shalt also decree a thing, and it shall be established unto thee: and the light shall shine upon thy ways."
-   Job 22:28

THOUGHTS OF IMPACT
Your Thoughts:

_____

_____

_____

_____

_____

_____

_____

_____

_____

_____

"Thou shalt also decree a thing, and it shall be established unto thee: and the light shall shine upon thy ways."
- Job 22:28

Day Ten

REFRESHING YOUR RELATIONSHIP WITH GOD

"You have said, 'Seek my face.' My heart says to you, 'Your face, Lord, do I seek.'"
- Psalms 27:8

From time to time in all our lives, our relationship with God grows cold. We do not have the same passion and the same intensity we once had when it comes to seeking His face and spending time with Him daily.

When our relationship with God grows stale, we run the risk of becoming spiritually weak, easily agitated, and unable to deal with many of the struggles of life that we must inevitably deal with on a day-to-day basis.

Our relationship with God empowers us with peace, joy, and happiness in the face of all adversity at all times of our lives. But none-the-less, we all have moments when our relationship with God is not as passionate or intimate as it once was.

You may be experiencing staleness in your relationship with God right now. If you find it challenging to spend time praying or reading the Word of God, your relationship with God has grown stale. If you look at spending time with God as a chore, and even when you spend time with Him, find that you do not get anything out of the experience, your relationship has grown stale.

What do we do when our relationship with God grows stale, and how do we refresh our relationship with Him? We must treat our relationship with God just as we would any intimate relationship.

Look at it this way; if you have a date night set up with your spouse or significant other, and you continuously do the same thing on your date night, eventually, the time you spend together will become sour and predictable. When the relationship becomes stale and predictable, you get no fulfillment out of it, and instead of growing closer together, you start to drift apart. You will eventually get to the place where you would rather stay home and do nothing rather than engage in the routineness of an unfulfilling date night.

With many of us, this is where we are in our relationship with God. It has become routine and predictable because we seek to engage Him and worship Him in a manner that has become routine and predictable. And because of that, we go unfulfilled in our personal devotion with God, and we stop spiritually growing because we are no longer getting into God's presence.

We pray because we feel like we are supposed to do as a good Christian, but we get nothing from it. No burdens are release from our shoulders. We read our Bible, but even that has become a chore, so we get no new profound revelations from it.

We would rather do anything else or nothing at all rather than continuing to experience another passionless date night with our God. We begin to say God isn't speaking to me or answering my prayers. We long to have the type of relationship with God that we see other Christians experiencing with Him.

But, just as we must add spice to our personal relationships to ensure we continue to enjoy the company of our spouses or significant other, we must add spice to our spiritual relationship with God. We must understand this fundamental fact about our devotion to God.

The key fact we must understand is that God wants us to enjoy our time with Him. When we set out to spend time with God, we must spend time with Him doing things we enjoy.

For so long, religion has programmed us to believe that the only way we are supposed to spend time with God is by reading the Bible or praying. But what happens when you do not feel like reading? What happenings when you feel as if you have nothing to say in prayer?

Many may find those statements puzzling, but if we are to engage God in a personal way and have a personal relationship, we must recognize that in our personal relationships, there comes a time when we want to spend time together. Still, we don't feel like verbally communicating.

There are periods when I want to spend time with my wife, but I do not really want to talk; I just want to be in her presence. The same is true with our relationship with God. There will be times when you do not feel like really communicating; you just want to be in His presence.

We need to add variety to our personal interactions with God so that our relationship never grows boring or stale.

- We can spend time with God listening to inspirational gospel music that helps to focus our attention on God.

- We can spend time with God writing our thoughts or feelings in a journal
- We can spend time with God by finding a quiet place to sit in His presence

The key thing here is if you are finding that you are not getting fulfillment from God in the time that you are spending with Him, and if your relationship is growing stale where you would rather be doing anything else than spending time with God, it is time to change how you and God spend time together.

Thought of Impact:

There's nothing wrong with establishing a set time to spend with God daily; that's the equivalent of having a standing date night in your relationship every Friday or Saturday night. Just change up what you do during that time from time to time to ensure that you and God are continuing to experience a fresh and fulfilling relationship that never gets boring, never grows stale, and is consistently filled with intimacy and passion.

THOUGHTS OF IMPACT
Your Thoughts:

_____

_____

_____

_____

_____

_____

_____

_____

_____

"You have said, 'Seek my face.' My heart says to you, 'Your face, Lord, do I seek.'
- Psalms 27:8

Your Thoughts:

_____

_____

_____

_____

_____

_____

_____

_____

_____

_____

"You have said, 'Seek my face.' My heart says to you, 'Your face, Lord, do I seek.'"
  - *Psalms 27:8*

Day Eleven

HAVING PURPOSE

"In the morning, as he was returning to the city, he became hungry. And seeing a fig tree by the wayside, he went to it and found nothing on it but only leaves. And he said to it, may no fruit ever come from you again. And the fig tree withered at once."

- *Matthew 21:18-19*

As Jesus went into the city, He got hungry. Seeing a fig tree, He went to get fruit from the tree to satisfy His hunger. However, the fig tree had no fruit leading Jesus to curse the fig tree declaring that from this point, no fruit will ever grow on the tree.

Many people have read this verse of scripture and wondered why Jesus cursed this fig tree. Since the fruit of the fig tree typically began to appear at the same time as the leaves, the fact that the leaves of this fig tree appeared to be in full bloom indicated the fruit on this tree was already growing.

However, upon arriving at the tree and seeing no fruit has grown, Jesus curses the tree. Jesus' actions have symbolic importance which signifies the hypocrisy of all who appear that they are bearing fruit but are not.

Like the fig tree, God created all of us with a purpose. We must examine ourselves and what we are doing in life to make sure we are bearing fruit related to the purpose that God created us for or if we will have the appearance of bearing fruit when we are not.

If we are not careful, we will live our lives trying to obtain the *"American Dream"* without placing focusing on the primary purpose for which God created us. God created us to give Him glory by serving Him in various capacities.

However, if we don't know in what capacity God wants us to serve Him, we could be presenting an image of bearing fruit when we are just a tree with fully bloomed leaves and no fruit.

When a tree such as a fig tree produces fruit, the fruit is not there for the tree to look beautiful. The fruit is there so that those who partake of the fruit produced by the tree can have sustenance that will help them maintain their life.

Our life is not about us; it is about fulfilling the purpose for which God created us because someone somewhere needs the fruit from within you that you should be producing to help them maintain their life.

God has also placed people in your life that should be producing good fruit that blesses your life. What they produce around you should build you up spiritually, encouraging and motivating you to pursue your destiny in God.

However, we have allowed too many people for far too long to remain planted around us with fully bloomed leaves and no fruit. They provide no sustenance to us but are a consistent drain to us. We must begin to take the mentality that Jesus took with the fig tree.

We must examine the people around us and identify the purpose they are supposed to be serving in our lives. If they are not producing fruit to meet that purpose, we must remove them from our inner circle so that God can replace them with someone who will.

But as you look to identify those in your circle who may need to be replaced, make sure that you are fulfilling your purpose in their lives.

Thought of Impact:

God created all of us for a purpose. Whatever your purpose, make sure that you are producing good fruit and not presenting the appearance of bearing good fruit. If you do not know your God-given purpose, I encourage you to seek God's face asking Him to reveal it to you. And remember, your purpose is never going to be about you, whatever it is; it is going to be about giving glory to God.

Your Thoughts:

_____

_____

_____

_____

_____

_____

_____

_____

_____

"In the morning, as he was returning to the city, he became hungry. And seeing a fig tree by the wayside, he went to it and found nothing on it but only leaves. And he said to it, may no fruit ever come from you again. And the fig tree withered at once."
- *Matthew 21:18-19*

THOUGHTS OF IMPACT
Your Thoughts:

_____

_____

_____

_____

_____

_____

_____

_____

_____

"In the morning, as he was returning to the city, he became hungry. And seeing a fig tree by the wayside, he went to it and found nothing on it but only leaves. And he said to it, may no fruit ever come from you again. And the fig tree withered at once."
- Matthew 21:18-19

Day Twelve

EXERCISING YOUR FAITH
Part I

"Have nothing to do with godless myths and old wives' tales; rather, train yourself to be godly. For physical training is of some value, but godliness has value for all things, holding promise for both the present life and the life to come."

- *1 Timothy 4:7-8 NIV*

The first thing we must understand about faith is that it is like a muscle. The more you use it, the stronger it becomes. We must also be aware that anything else we feed that is not of faith also becomes stronger.

In the scripture, Paul says we are to have nothing to do with godless myths and old wives' tales. Well, what are godless myths and old wives' tales? They are silly stories that get dressed up as *"religion."*

These are practices and beliefs that people have done, continue to do, and are passed down from generation to generation that has no value or truth in them. They seem to be valid, but they are demonic in nature, designed to put you in bondage and keep you in bondage. Many times, we place more trust in these superstitious beliefs than we do our faith in God, and because of that, these myths and old wives' tales become stronger and have a greater influence in our lives and over our lives.

For instance, many of us may be familiar with and heard the myth or old wives' tale that you will have seven years of bad luck of you break a mirror. Many of us have broken our share of mirrors during our lifetime, and we have all had our share of what could be considered bad luck. However, the two things have no relationship with each other. Now, whether *you* ever believed that myth to be true, there are many people who have thought it to be true.

Because they believed they would have bad luck when they accidentally broke the glass of a mirror, they spent seven years of their life in bondage, believing that every bad thing that was happening to them during that period of time could be attributed to them breaking a mirror.

We have also gone through seasons where people placed a lot of value in horoscopes believing their zodiac sign signified what type of personality or temperament they would have as well as the personality or temperament of someone else. There are instances where women and men have turned down what could have been an promising relationship simply because their horoscope said "Capricorns and Libra's" are not compatible. Some people have entered relationships because they believed since their signs were compatible, it was a sign they should be together, and they have probably experienced a relationship filled with more drama than they could imagine.

The Bible declares that horoscopes and astrology seek to predict future events an influence people's behavior and should be considered a form of sorcery that is abominable to God and is to be avoided by the people of God.

The scripture tells us that godliness is what we should place our focus on as it is more profitable in every way of our life. In this verse of scripture, godliness is defined as *"spiritual training,"* meaning exercising our faith.

The more we exercise our faith, the stronger it becomes. We need to move past worrying about the small things in our life. Worrying about small things in our life is a sign that our faith is weak. For instance, a person who works out often can go into the gym, and there are certain exercises and a certain amount of weight they have no concern about lifting because they have been working out long enough to know they can handle it.

However, someone who has not worked out as long may be the same size, but their muscles are not trained or conditioned to handle the same workout. The same is true with faith. You may have been saved for 30 years, but if you rarely exercise your faith, a person whose been saved five years and exercises their faith daily will be spiritually stronger.

We need to work on exercising our faith daily so that standing on the Word of God will be the first thing we lean on rather than vain and useless superstitions.

Thought of Impact:

Over the next few chapters, we will talk about Exercising our Faith. Often, we hear about using our faith, but many people do not understand faith, nor do they know how to use it. God gave us a powerful weapon with faith, but we will continue to be defeated in spiritual warfare if we do not know how to use it. My prayer is that once we complete this discussion, you will begin to consistently grow and exercise your faith.

THOUGHTS OF IMPACT
Your Thoughts:

_____

_____

_____

_____

_____

_____

_____

_____

_____

"Have nothing to do with godless myths and old wives' tales; rather, train yourself to be godly. For physical training is of some value, but godliness has value for all things, holding promise for both the present life and the life to come."
- *1 Timothy 4:7-8 NIV*

Your Thoughts:

_____

_____

_____

_____

_____

_____

_____

_____

_____

"Have nothing to do with godless myths and old wives' tales; rather, train yourself to be godly. For physical training is of some value, but godliness has value for all things, holding promise for both the present life and the life to come."
- *1 Timothy 4:7-8 NIV*

THOUGHTS OF IMPACT

EXERCISING YOUR FAITH
Part 2

"And as soon as those bearing the ark had come as far as the Jordan, and the feet of the priests bearing the ark were dipped in the brink of the water, the waters coming down from above stood and rose up in a heap very far away"

- *Joshua 3:15-16*

God tells Joshua that He will show the people of Israel that just as He was with Moses, He is also with Joshua.

As God is about to lead the people of Israel into the Promised Land, He tells Joshua to command the priest to carry the Ark of the Covenant and stand in the Jordan River.

Joshua and Israel know is that standing between them and the Promised Land was the Jordan River. During this time of the season, the Jordan River was higher than usual and overflowing more than usual because it was harvest time, and the region was experiencing an increase in rain.

Joshua gathers all the people together, preparing to cross over the Jordan, and he commands the priest to carry the Ark of the Covenant and stand in the Jordan. As the soles of the feet of the priest carrying the Ark of the Covenant were submerged into the waters of the Jordan River; the waters stopped flowing and parted so that the Israelites could cross over on dry ground just as they did when Moses parted the Red Sea.

When we look at this situation, we learn key steps from Joshua on how to exercise our faith. The first thing we must understand is that Joshua knew the promise of God. God had promised Joshua and all of Israel that He would deliver them to the Promised Land, a Land of Inheritance. Joshua also saw an obstacle standing between them and the Promised Land, the Jordan River.

Joshua knew for God to keep His promise and deliver them to the Promised Land, God would have to remove the obstacle, which was the Jordan River, from their path.

THOUGHTS OF IMPACT

The second thing we see from Joshua is that he received a Word from God. God told Him when the soles of the priest's feet carrying the Ark of the Covenant entered the Jordan; the waters would be cut off from flowing.

The third thing we must realize when it comes to exercising our faith is that whatever God tells us to do, we must understand that He is going with us. The Ark of the Covenant signified the presence of God amongst His people. When the priest stepped into the Jordan carrying the Ark, they were stepping out on faith, and they were carrying God with them.

From Joshua and the Israelites situations of crossing the Jordan River, we too can learn how to exercise our faith. The first thing we need to do to exercise our faith is to know the promises of God. The promises of God are found in the Word of God. When we know what God promises us, we have greater confidence that no matter what obstacles are standing in our way, God will remove them in order to keep His promise.

The second thing we must do to exercise our faith is to get a Word from God. Once we know what God has promised us, for us to remove the obstacles hindering us from receiving what belongs to us, we must receive instruction and direction from God on how to proceed. This is where many of us fail. We know the promises of God, but we never seek God to get a word of direction from Him so that He can lead us to overcome the obstacles standing in our way to receive the promise.

Before God spoke to Joshua, Joshua began directing the people of Israel in worship, telling them to consecrate themselves to God, which is to set yourself aside for God, focusing solely on Him rather than anything else going on in your life. As the people and Joshua began setting themselves aside to worship, God began to speak. To receive direction from God, we must begin setting ourselves aside at times to focus solely on Him so that He can direct our paths.

The third thing we need to do to exercise our faith is to step out and do what God has instructed us to do, whether we agree with it or not. During this time of the season, the Jordan River was not a gentle river with waters gently flowing like a stream. The waves were violently crashing all around with roaring winds, ready to overtake anything that tried to settle on the waters.

But just as the priest was carrying God with them by way of the Ark of the Covenant, we too carry God with us when we step on in faith by way of the Holy Spirit.

God did not tell the priest to try to hold back the waters; He did not tell them to dig a trench to re-direct the flow of the water. He did not tell them anything that made sense to the natural mind. He told them to go stand in the river, and He took care of the rest.

When it comes to exercising our faith, let us first know what God has promised us; let us then seek His face for direction on how to position ourselves to receive what He has promised us and let us step out and do what He has instructed us to do to receive our promise trusting that He will remove any and all obstacles standing in opposition to us.

Thought of Impact:

Before the Jordan River stopped flowing, the people had to first put their foot in the water. Before the obstacles stop flowing in your life, you first must go stand your ground amid them and trust God to do the rest.

THOUGHTS OF IMPACT
Your Thoughts:

_____

_____

_____

_____

_____

_____

_____

_____

_____

_____

"And as soon as those bearing the ark had come as far as the Jordan, and the feet of the priests bearing the ark were dipped in the brink of the water, the waters coming down from above stood and rose up in a heap very far away"
- Joshua 3:15-16

Your Thoughts:

_____

_____

_____

_____

_____

_____

_____

_____

_____

"And as soon as those bearing the ark had come as far as the Jordan, and the feet of the priests bearing the ark were dipped in the brink of the water, the waters coming down from above stood and rose up in a heap very far away"
- *Joshua 3:15-16*

THOUGHTS OF IMPACT

21 Thoughts to Impact Your Life

EXERCISING YOUR FAITH
PART 3

"Knowing this, that the trying of your faith works patience. But let patience have her perfect work, that you may be perfect and entire wanting nothing"

- *James 1:3-4*

When we talk about exercising our faith, one of the main things we lack as Christians is patience. We believe that if the promise of God says this and I begin exercising my faith to receive it, then it should happen instantaneously. In some cases, we will receive the fulfillment of what God promised us quickly when we begin standing on faith.

However, most times in our lives we should not expect instantaneous manifestation. In the scripture, we are told that *"the trying of our faith works patience and we are to let patience have her perfect work."* It sounds good, but what does it mean?

In simple terms, it means we need to grow to a point where we patiently trust God to fulfill His promises no matter what. That sounds good too, but what does that really mean? In many of our circumstances, we can all say that we believed we were trusting God no matter what the obstacles we faced. So, let us break this scripture down to understand how it applies in real-life situations. To do this, I want to talk to you from the book of Daniel for a moment.

In the book of Daniel, God gives Daniel a prophetic vision in a dream. The dream scares Daniel even though Daniel doesn't know what the dream means. So, Daniel prays to God to send him the ability to interpret the prophetic dream he had.

As Daniel is waiting to understand this dream, he does not eat or drink anything for three weeks. Then an angel arrives to give Daniel an understanding of the dream. Before the angel tells Daniel what the vision means, he tells Daniel on the day you first humbled yourself and prayed to ask for revelation, God heard your words and granted your request. He tells Daniel that for 21 days, he was trying to get to Daniel to bring him what he asked for but was held up by a demonic force attempting to block Daniel from receiving an understanding of his dream (*See Daniel Chapter 10*).

The Bible says we are to approach the Throne of Grace boldly and make our request known to God (*See Hebrews 4:16*). What we must take from Daniel's situation is that the moment we humble ourselves in prayer and approach the Throne of Grace and make our request known to God, God grants our request right then.

When we make our request known to God, if what we are asking Him is in line with His Word, God's answer is always yes. God has no desire to tell us no under the New Covenant (*See 2 Corinthians 1:20*). So why have I not received the things for which I have prayed?

You may not have received it for one of two reasons.

- Reason One: Either your request does not line up with God's Word.
- Two: You have not allowed patience to have its perfect work.

See, when we ask for something, the Bible tells us there are demonic forces seeking to block us from receiving it.

This is why God says we are to be patient and allow patience to perfect us that we may be complete and lack nothing.

Let us look at it like this. You pray to God, saying, Lord, I want a new five-bedroom home, with a two-car garage, built-in office, walk-in closets, Jacuzzi bathtubs, and marble floors. Lord, I need the money to be able to pay for this house. You pray that request to God. God answers your request right then with a Yes.

Now, what we are expecting is money to fall into our hands right then and a house with the exact specifications to jump out at us all within the span of a day. But that is not going to happen. Once God says yes, demonic forces are going to try to block us from receiving what we asked.

In most cases, we will find the house, but we will not have the money. So, we will revert to that old false teaching saying God said no. "*Well, it's just not the Lord's will.*" Well, the Lords will say, "I came that you may have life and life more abundantly" (*See John 10:10*). The Lords will say, "*Whatever you ask in my name I will do it*" (*See John 14:13*). The Lord's will say, "*For as many as are the promises of God, in Christ, they are [all answered] 'Yes.' So, through Him, we say our 'Amen' to the glory of God"* (See 2 Corinthians 1:20).

What has happened is the enemy is holding up the financial fulfillment of the blessing to hinder you from receiving the full manifestation of what you asked. Looking back at the text. The scripture says, *"let patience have her perfect work that you may be perfect, complete and lacking nothing."*

Using our example, if we found the house but do not have the money, we are incomplete and lacking money. If we have the money but cannot find the house, we can buy any house, but it is not the house we wanted, so the fulfillment is not perfect.

I need you to get that because so many times, we have settled for stuff that was just *O.K.* because we were not patient enough to wait on God to bring us perfection. Perfection in the sense that the fulfillment reflected our request.

But what happens when we do not have the money nor the house. We again start questioning whether God has told us no. After an extended period, we give up asking God and believing we will never receive it and doubt kills faith.

So, as those angels are fighting against demonic forces to bring manifestation to what you first asked for, once you begin to doubt, God has no choice but to cancel the fulfillment of your request because it has no place to go. Not because God said no. Not because God could not, would not, or did not provide it, but because we did not allow patience to maintain our faith.

When the scripture says we are to let patience have her perfect work, it means that our faith should remain constant and unchanging. Remember what Jesus said about faith being as a mustard seed (*See Matthew 17:20*)? The mustard seed does not change regardless of what else is going on in the garden where it is planted.

Now there are some cases where you may have to wait years for the fulfillment of your request or for what God has told you. But your faith must remain constant and ready to receive without doubt. Israel waited hundreds of years for the Land of Inheritance; David was anointed King but had to wait almost 30 years before he could take the throne; Jesus confounded the religious leaders of his time at the age of 12 but still had to wait another 18 years to begin his ministry. So, let us too be patient.

Thought of Impact:

Patience makes our faith just like the mustard seed, unchanged by what is going on around us but constant and enduring. So, as we begin exercising our faith, we must learn the virtue of patience. Rather than getting antsy and start doubting God, let patience have her perfect work that we may be perfect, entire and complete, lacking nothing.

Your Thoughts:

"Knowing this, that the trying of your faith works patience. But let patience have her perfect work, that you may be perfect and entire wanting nothing"
- James 1:3-4

THOUGHTS OF IMPACT

Your Thoughts:

_____

_____

_____

_____

_____

_____

_____

_____

_____

"Knowing this, that the trying of your faith works patience. But let patience have her perfect work, that you may be perfect and entire wanting nothing"
- James 1:3-4

Day Fifteen

EXERCISING YOUR FAITH
Part 4

"So, also faith by itself, if it does not have works, is dead."

- *James 2:17*

In the scripture, James tells us that if we see a brother or sister in Christ wearing old clothes and they do not have anything to eat, to tell them that God is going to bless them is useless.

Why is this useless? This is useless because God is not going to step out of Heaven with a new set of clothes to put on their body or a warm plate of food to feed them. God is going to provide them what they need through the Body of Christ, meaning through their fellow brothers and sisters in Christ. God does His work through us, so to tell them God will provide without us doing our part to assist them in getting what they need is useless. We are telling them God will provide without doing our part of allowing God to provide for them through us.

James says just as it is useless to tell them that God is going to provide for them without positioning ourselves to allow God to work through us, faith without works by us is also useless.

As Christians, we have done a good job telling God what we need, but we place the burden on Him to do everything by Himself. We have taken faith to the extreme in some sense by placing the complete burden on God without taking any of the responsibility ourselves.

For instance, if we are trying to find employment and we pray for God to let us find a job, but we cannot sit back and wait for someone to call us. We cannot say God is going to give me a job, but we never fill out an application or never send out a resume. We are professing our faith for God to provide us with a job, but we are not taking any action to position ourselves for Him to do so.

It is only when we fill out the application or send out the resume that the favor of God can begin working on our behalf to allow our application or resume to stand out amongst the hundreds or thousands of others that are sitting on the hiring manager's desk.

If you are believing that God is going to allow you to start and have a successful business, there comes a time when you have to put some action behind what you are believing and what you are professing; otherwise, your faith is useless or dead.

When James says faith without works is dead, he is saying there is no life in what we believe. If there was life in what we profess we are believing God for, we will begin working on it to bring it to fruition. Previously I told you the story of Joshua telling the priest to carry the Ark of the Covenant and go stand in the Jordan River.

The Jordan River would have never parted for the people to walk across on dry land if the priest never stepped foot into the water. The things we are asking God for and the things God has told us we can have will never happen if we never take the necessary steps to begin the process.

What is it that you are believing God for in your life? Have you taken the steps to begin the process, or are you waiting for God to do all the work? If you're waiting for God to do all the work, you will never have what you desire. But if you begin taking the steps, God will empower you; God will open doors for you, God will move obstacles from in front of you, God will fight against the enemy to protect you, and God will prosper you to ensure your eventual success.

Does this mean there will not be a setback? No! Does this mean I will not fail sometimes? No! Failure is a teacher sometimes. This means that the finished outcome that God promised you will be received no matter what setbacks you must experience and no matter what failures you must experience.

The Bible says that when Moses parted the Red Sea, the Israelites crossed over on dry ground. The Bible also says when the Jordan River was parted, the Israelites crossed over on dry ground. The Bible does not say that they did not feel the breeze of the wind blowing in their face as He kept the waters parted; the Bible does not say that they did not feel drops of water spraying in their face as they crossed over.

Even though God is going with us, will open doors for us, and will protect us, when we step out on faith, it does not mean walking through the door is going to be easy; it does not mean that we will not get hit by the enemy as God protects us. It means that what God promised us will be fulfilled if we first put some action behind what we say we believe.

Thought of Impact:

Faith without works is dead, so whatever you are believing God for or are asking God to do on your behalf, once you pray and ask, begin taking the necessary steps that will allow God to go to work on your behalf. Anyone can say they believe, but a genuine believer steps out on what they profess to believe.

THOUGHTS OF IMPACT
Your Thoughts:

_____

_____

_____

_____

_____

_____

_____

_____

_____

"So, also faith by itself, if it does not have works, is dead."
- James 2:17

Your Thoughts:

_____

_____

_____

_____

_____

_____

_____

_____

_____

_____

"So, also faith by itself, if it does not have works, is dead."
- James 2:17

Day Sixteen

STRETCHED TO THE NEXT LEVEL

Part 1

"Now the Lord said to Abram, 'Go from your country and your kindred and your father's house to the land that I will show you.'"

- *Genesis 12:1*

There are times in our life when God is calling us away from the known and the comfortable just as He did Abram. However, rather than stepping into the unknown, we try to hold on to the things God wants us to release.

When we look at God's call to Abram, He tells him to leave his country. This means leave the place you know as home, get away from the comforts of familiar surroundings. If we stay in comfortable and familiar surroundings, we limit ourselves from the possibility of stepping into the place of unexpected blessings.

Familiar surroundings are just that, familiar and predictable. Nothing new happens in familiar surroundings; if something new happened, it would not be considered familiar. It is the familiarity that makes it comfortable. However, if we are consumed with predictability, we are not able to receive anything new and unexpected from God.

When we live our lives knowing exactly what the day has in store for us, our mindset begins to limit us to expect to have the same experiences as yesterday. Since we are stuck in yesterday, we are not receptive to a today move from God. God operates in the unexpected, and the only way to experience God in a new way is to get out of the comforts of the expected and into the uncomfortable-ness of the unexpected.

The first thing God tells Abram to do is get away from familiar surroundings. God is saying if I can get you to change your scenery where you begin to see something new daily, you will develop an expectation of having unexpected experiences daily. Once God can get you to begin expecting the unexpected by changing your scenery, He can give you a new vision for your life.

If there are places in our life that have become familiar and predictable, we need to begin listening for God to tell us to move. If we remain in predictable situations in our life, we cannot expect God to show up with unexpected blessings. God will not do the unexpected in a place where your mindset has limited you to expect the routine.

Thought of Impact:

I encourage you today when you hear the voice of God and the leading of the Holy Spirit trying to direct you to divert from what is familiar and what is comfortable to venture out into the unknown and uncomfortable; Go!

Step out in faith, trusting God to lead you, protect, you and provide for you. Lean on God because He and He alone is your source.

Your Thoughts:

_____

_____

_____

_____

_____

_____

_____

_____

_____

"Now the Lord said to Abram, 'Go from your country and your kindred and your father's house to the land that I will show you.'"
- *Genesis 12:1*

THOUGHTS OF IMPACT
Your Thoughts:

_____

_____

_____

_____

_____

_____

_____

_____

_____

"Now the Lord said to Abram, 'Go from your country and your kindred and your father's house to the land that I will show you.'"
- *Genesis 12:1*

Day Seventeen

STRETCHED TO THE NEXT LEVEL
Part 2

"Now the Lord said to Abram, 'Go from your country and your kindred and your father's house to the land that I will show you.'"

- Genesis 12:1

As we previously discussed, there are many times in our lives that God may be calling us away from the known and the comfortable, but rather than stepping into the unknown, we try to hold on to exactly what God wants us to release.

When God told Abram to leave his country, He was telling him to leave the comforts and predictability of his familiar surroundings. We too must leave the comforts of our familiar surroundings so that our mindset is not limited to expecting the same experiences of yesterday, blocking God's ability to do something new in our lives.

The next thing God told Abram to do was to get away from his kindred. God not only wants Abram to separate himself from the familiarity of his surroundings, but He also wants him to separate himself from the familiarity of the people around him

We must realize there are people in our lives who are not doing anything with their own life. In some cases, they may be doing something with their life, but they are not moving in the same direction in which God is trying to move us.

When we have a desire to go to another level, we must understand that in order to get there, rather than surrounding ourselves with people who continuously operate on the same level of predictability, we must begin surrounding ourselves with people who are striving to go higher as well as those who are already operating at the level we desire to reach.

If we remain around the same people engaging in the same activities, having the same conversations, our minds are never challenged to explore new possibilities. Just as God uses us to be a blessing and an influence in the lives of others, He will use other people to be a blessing and an influence in our lives.

However, if our mindsets are limited to the predictable familiarity of the people around us, we are not able to receive anything new from them because we do not have a level of expectation to receive anything new from them.

God wants us to begin surrounding ourselves with new people who are doing the things He is leading us to do, as well as surround ourselves with others who are striving in our direction. When we get away from the comforts of the familiar people around us into the uncomfortable and unexpectedness of new people, we develop a mindset to expect something from them that we have never experienced before.

Once our mindset begins to expect new experiences from new people, God can begin blessing us with unexpected blessings from unexpected people. But it all starts with us getting out of our comfort zones, getting away from familiarity, and allowing God to direct our paths to new places and new people.

The next thing that God tells Abram is to get away from his father's house. As long as Abram lived in his father's house, it was his father's responsibility to provide for him, protect him and cover him spiritually. However, until we step out on our own to make our own way in the world, we will never get a revelation of who God is for ourselves.

As long as Abram stayed in his father's house, he would only know God through his father's revelation. We can take our children to church and teach them about God, but it is not until they go out into the world and earn a living for themselves that they get to know God as a provider.

For us to get to a new level, we must have a new revelation of God. The only way to get a new revelation of God is to leave the comforts of predictable familiarity and step out into the unknown and uncomfortable. When we step into the unknown and uncomfortable, God can reveal himself to us in a new way through our new experiences.

This is how we grow more intimately with God. We must not be afraid of new experiences, meeting new people, and going to new places because it is only through the newness of life and the newness of experiences that we get to see God in a new way.

If we embrace the comforts of home without venturing out into the world, God cannot open our minds to receive a new vision for our lives.

If we embrace the same conversations on the same level with the same people without meeting new people and engaging in new conversations to expand our horizons, God cannot open our minds to receive new wisdom.

If we depend on others rather than depending on God, we cannot experience a new revelation of God because we will only know God through how He has revealed Himself to other people with no real experiences with Him for ourselves. Let us step out of our comfort zones and allow God to stretch us to a new level with new experiences.

Thought of Impact:

Don't get comfortable where you are; embrace something new. God said, "Watch, I am about to do something new... (*See Isaiah 43:19*)." But He can only do something new when we are willing to leave what is old.

THOUGHTS OF IMPACT
Your Thoughts:

_____

_____

_____

_____

_____

_____

_____

_____

_____

"Now the Lord said to Abram, 'Go from your country and your kindred and your father's house to the land that I will show you.'"
Genesis 12:1

21 Thoughts to Impact Your Life

Your Thoughts:

___

___

___

___

___

___

___

___

___

"Now the Lord said to Abram, 'Go from your country and your kindred and your father's house to the land that I will show you.'"

Genesis 12:1

THOUGHTS OF IMPACT

Day Eighteen

STRETCHED TO THE NEXT LEVEL
Part 3

"And I will make of you a great nation, and I will bless you and make your name great, so that you will be a blessing."

- *Genesis 12:2*

Over the last few chapters, we have discussed that God wants us to get away from our familiar surroundings so that our mindset is not limited to only expecting the same experiences of yesterday which block us from expecting God to do something new in our lives today.

We also discussed that we must begin surrounding ourselves with new people; people who are striving to go to the next level in their relationship with God, striving to be entrepreneur's, striving to go to another level so that we do not become complacent where we are because of the company we keep.

We must also step out of our comfort zone depending on others and begin relying solely on God. When we get out of the comfortable into the uncomfortable, we can get a new revelation of God for ourselves.

For leaving the known and the comfortable for the unknown and uncomfortable, what can we trust God to do for us? Well, God says for being obedient to the call to leave the known for the unknown, He would make Abram a great nation.

From Abram's perspective we must understand that before Israel became the nation it is today, it was first considered to be Abram's family. This tells us is that we must not always look for God to provide blessings just for us because that is temporal or temporary thinking.

Sometimes, God is setting us up so that He can be a blessing to our bloodline for generations to come. The Nation of Israel stands today because of Abram's faithfulness about 4000 years ago.

Look at what God is doing in your life from a long-term perspective and not shortsightedly. For instance, God may be urging you to step out and start a business. You may struggle and toil over that business and only see small gains till the day you die. However, because you step out on faith at God's call to leave the comfortable for the unknown and the uncomfortable, God could raise your business to be one of the largest, most respected, and most profitable in its industry and serve as a financial blessing to your family who now owns and runs the business for generations to come all because of your faithfulness.

Many times, the thought of living on a tight budget takes us out of our comfort zone because we are used to spending what we have whenever we desire. However, if God is calling us to leave what we are used to for what we are not used to, we may not experience the full effects of the blessings, but our family may.

When we change our spending habits and our attitude about finances, we may spend the rest of our lives working ourselves out of debt. But because we heeded the call of God, He allows the next generation of our bloodline to develop the good budgeting and spending habits we took and avoid ever being in bondage to debt.

God told Abram if you leave what you know for what you do not yet know; if you leave what you expect for what is unexpected, and if you leave what is comfortable for what is uncomfortable, I promise you your family will reap the *good harvest* from your fruits of labor.

Thought of Impact:

Let us begin heeding God's call to get from where we are so that He can make our family, *our* future bloodline great.

Your Thoughts:

_____

_____

_____

_____

_____

_____

_____

_____

_____

"And I will make of you a great nation, and I will bless you and make your name great, so that you will be a blessing."
- *Genesis 12:2*

THOUGHTS OF IMPACT

Your Thoughts:

_____

_____

_____

_____

_____

_____

_____

_____

_____

_____

"And I will make of you a great nation, and I will bless you and make your name great, so that you will be a blessing."
- *Genesis 12:2*

Day Nineteen

STRETCHED TO THE NEXT LEVEL
Part 4

"And I will make of you a great nation, and I will bless you and make your name great, so that you will be a blessing."

- *Genesis 12:2*

Previously we discussed that there are times when God is trying to move us in a new direction not necessarily where we may get to see the benefits of our labors but that we may lay the foundation for the future generations of our bloodline to build and be blessed by God.

God then tells Abram that I will bless you and make your name great, so that you will be a blessing. It is vitally important to understand why God stretches us to new and higher levels and pours an abundance of blessings into our lives.

In order to go to another level, you must understand your purpose for being there. The reason God desires to stretch us to another level and give us an abundance of favor like we have never seen before is not so we can sit back and live the easy life. The reason God takes us to another level is so that we can become better servants to others.

Jesus said that the greatest among you shall be the servant of all (*See Matthew 23:11*). This is why God tells Abram I will bless you and make your name great, so that you will be a blessing. What God is saying is I will bless you so that you can become a blessing to others.

Many times, we take a limited view of the success we have in life. We sit back, looking at the fruits of our labors, saying, *"I worked hard to get to where I am, and if I did, others can do it too."* However, we dismiss the fact that God is the one who blessed us; God is the one who opened doors of opportunity, making it possible for us to be successful. God is the one who touched the hearts of others to mentor us and show favor toward us. And now, God is the one who has placed us in a position of authority or influence so that He can work His purposes through us to bless others the same way we were blessed ourselves.

When God raises us to another level, we are responsible for reaching our hands back to help pull up others. When God blesses us with more than enough, it is our responsibility to put the overflow to work, fulfilling God's purposes as the Holy Spirit directs us.

Abram left all that he knew of his home life, family, and friends and ventured out into the unknown as God led him. When Abram reached the land that God promised him, it was nothing more than a land of wilderness with other people living in a place that Abram could not legally make a claim. However, for being faithful, God blessed Abram so that as his new nation began to grow by first having a child in his old age. Abram knew that where God was taking him was not about him but about him laying a foundation that would be a blessing to the people who would come after him.

As God raises us up, let us not be short-sighted in our thinking. Let us not become consumed with believing that God just wants to bless *us*. Let us realize that God has placed us in a position to reach our hands out to bless someone else who is in need, to speak wisdom to someone who may be going through something you have already overcome.

Wherever God leads you in your life, know that He's leading you there to bless you so that you can be a blessing to others.

Thought of Impact:

We cannot continue doing the same thing expecting different results. For us to experience something new from God, we must begin leaving our comfort zones and connecting with new people to be introduced to new and different perspectives. Challenge yourself to get comfortable being uncomfortable to experience God in exciting new ways. Open your mind to the possibility that God not only wants to bless you but others through you. When we allow God to stretch us to the next level, we will experience a life filled with possibility and excitement.

Your Thoughts:

_____

_____

_____

_____

_____

_____

_____

_____

"And I will make of you a great nation, and I will bless you and make your name great, so that you will be a blessing."
- *Genesis 12:2*

THOUGHTS OF IMPACT
Your Thoughts:

_____

_____

_____

_____

_____

_____

_____

_____

_____

"And I will make of you a great nation, and I will bless you and make your name great, so that you will be a blessing."
- *Genesis 12:2*

Day Twenty

SPIRITUAL FULLNESS

"I want to begin by reading to you this morning from the book of Ephesians. And it says, "Now to him who is able to do far more abundantly than all that we ask or think, according to the power at work within us."

- *Ephesians 3:20 ESV*

So often in our lives, we hear about the great things in the Bible that have been done by faith. We look at those Biblical events as great stories without realizing that even though those events may have happened thousands of years ago, those people were regular people just like you and me.

There was nothing spectacular about them; there was nothing special about them that made God say, let Me place them on some pedestal and grant them amazing power that will be out of reach for everyone else.

Biblical heroes such as Moses, Elijah, Peter, and Paul were regular people like you and me. They had faults and bad habits. Their life before entering a relationship with God was far from perfect.

Moses and Paul were both murderers, Elijah suffered bouts of depression, and Peter used profanity and even denied Jesus out of fear for his own life. Even though these men suffered from these tremendous faults, God could still work miracles and accomplish His purpose through their lives.

We may look at our lives and look at the routine of it and believe we have nothing to offer to God or to the Kingdom, but God has a purpose for your life. God has something that He desires to do through you to help build His kingdom and give Him glory.
However, we limit ourselves to what God can do through us because we consistently disqualify ourselves based on our faults. We say things like:

- I drunk a beer last night, so God can't use me today

- I didn't pray enough this morning, so the Spirit of God probably won't speak to me

- Other Christians are doing great things, but I can't think of anything to do for God that will make a difference

We disqualify ourselves from the work of the Kingdom instead of trusting in God's Grace, His unmerited favor that tells us that God does not depend on us to do anything to qualify ourselves for service. The only thing required of us is to simply believe in Him and His ability to do anything through us, not because we've done anything good to qualify ourselves but because He loves us.

When we begin to place our trust in God and His ability to operate through us, we'll begin to see that God is truly able to do exceedingly, abundantly, above all we can ask or think according to the power that is at work within us.

When we came to Jesus, God endowed us with Power. And that power can do anything because it belongs to Him and operates according to His ability, not ours. Since it operates according to His ability and not ours, we should begin to trust that through us, God can do anything.

When people are sick, we should no longer doubt our ability to lay our hands on them, pray for them and expect them to get well. We should no longer doubt our ability to speak into the atmosphere something positive over our life and over our family and expect to see it come to pass.

We must remember that the power at work within us is God's power operating according to His abilities and not our own. When we get ourselves out of the way and begin to walk in faith trusting God, we'll begin to see Him do exceedingly; abundantly above all we can ask or think according to the power He has placed within us.

Thought of Impact:

When we focus on ourselves and what we lack, we begin to doubt what God can do. We must keep our eyes off ourselves and keep them focused on Jesus. When we focus on Jesus, we will

no longer doubt what's possible, but we will believe that anything is possible.

21 Thoughts to Impact Your Life

Your Thoughts:

"I want to begin by reading to you this morning from the book of Ephesians. And it says, "Now to him who is able to do far more abundantly than all that we ask or think, according to the power at work within us."
Ephesians 3:20 ESV

THOUGHTS OF IMPACT
Your Thoughts:

_____

_____

_____

_____

_____

_____

_____

_____

_____

_____

"I want to begin by reading to you this morning from the book of Ephesians. And it says, "Now to him who is able to do far more abundantly than all that we ask or think, according to the power at work within us."
Ephesians 3:20 ESV

Day Twenty-One

PURSUING YOUR DESTINY

"For I know the plans I have for you, declares the Lord, plans to prosper you and not to harm you, plans to give you hope and a future."

- Jeremiah 29:11 NIV

If there is one thing you can be sure about in this world, it is that God has a plan for your life. God has a plan in mind for you that does not involve your life being filled with turmoil but peace, not consumed with disasters but blessings.

God desires a life for us that is filled with more prosperity and pleasure than we could ever imagine. Now the question arises in our minds; if God desires so much for me and my life, why do I have to deal with turmoil and disaster? Why must I face hardships and displeasures in my life?

In order to understand the significance of your struggle, you need not look any further than a seed. A seed is planted in the earth, under the dirt and the soil. However, the seed is just a seed, it has a purpose, but the seed is not yet ready to be on the outside what it is on the inside.

In the ground, the seed is watered and nourished until it breaks out of its shell. Once that seed breaks free from its shell, it establishes a root within the dirt that will continue to nourish it. Once free from the shell with an established root, it must fight and push and squirm and struggle until it breaks itself free from under the soil.

Breaking free from the soil, whatever was once in the seed, whatever it was destined to be, now stands proud and tall for all the world to see. It does not hide, it does not feel shame, and it knows it has a right to be admired by all creation because it has been rightfully established on the earth with every push, squirm and struggle it took to break free from the dirt of the earth. And because it has its root established in the dirt, it never forgets where it came from, neither does it forget from where the source of the nourishment which sustains its life flow.

Just as this seed has something on the inside of it that it is destined to be, God has placed destiny inside of us. God has destiny written all over your life. But just as the seed had its purpose on the inside but was not quite ready to show it, we too may not be ready to stand in our purpose or our destiny.

We must establish a root in the soil of the Word of God so that we never forget that God is our source and the sustainer of our life, and all that we are flows from Him. We must fight, push, squirm and struggle against the attacks of the enemy as we Pursue our Destiny.

But once we reach our destiny; reach our purpose, we can stand proud and tall knowing I deserve the Favor that God has placed upon me, I deserve the Blessings that God has ordained for my life, and I deserved all the good things that He promised me in His Word. Not because I did anything so great or so grand, but because I placed my trust in Him and allowed Him to mold, form, and shape me into what He desired me to be.

Thought of Impact:

We must Pursue our Destiny by Pursuing God. As we pursue Him, we must allow Him to grow us as He would grow a flower out of the ground of the earth. We must let Him water us, nourish us and groom us. And when the time comes, we must fight to remain faithful to what God has created us to be and not transformed into what the World desires us to be.

Your Thoughts:

"For I know the plans I have for you, declares the Lord, plans to prosper you and not to harm you, plans to give you hope and a future."
Jeremiah 29:11 NIV

THOUGHTS OF IMPACT

Your Thoughts:

_____

_____

_____

_____

_____

_____

_____

_____

_____

_____

"For I know the plans I have for you, declares the Lord, plans to prosper you and not to harm you, plans to give you hope and a future."
Jeremiah 29:11 NIV

Your Thoughts:

THOUGHTS OF IMPACT
Your Thoughts:

Your Thoughts:

THOUGHTS OF IMPACT
Your Thoughts:

Your Thoughts:

THOUGHTS OF IMPACT
Your Thoughts:

Your Thoughts:

THOUGHTS OF IMPACT
Your Thoughts:

Your Thoughts:

ABOUT THE AUTHOR

Apostle Darrius Geter is the Founder & Overseer of Full Impact Christian Church and has been preaching the Gospel for over ten years. Apostle Geter has a desire to see God's people grow in authority by applying the Word of God to their lives. He is a graduate of Georgia Southern University, has an MBA, and earned his Master of Divinity from Luther Rice Seminary, where he is also a doctoral candidate.

Apostle Geter is the author of the life-changing books *"Violent Faith: It's Time to Get Violent!"* and *"Identity: You're Not Who You Pretend to Be,"* and co-author of various other works.

In addition to writing life empowering books and various speaking engagements, Apostle Geter is the Founder of Darrius Geter Ministries and The Full Impact Foundation, whose mission is to Edify, Educate, and Empower by providing college scholarships to first-time students, promoting entrepreneurship and economic development in low-income communities while serving as an advocate to address social issues that plague communities.

Apostle Geter is married to Prophetess Dayvener Geter, and together they have four beautiful daughters.

Books by Darrius Geter

Violent Faith: It's Time to Get Violent!

Identity: You're Not Who You Pretend to Be

Transforming Your Thought into a Plan (Co-Author)

The Shift: Seeking Heaven's Involvement for Transition (Co-Author)

Social Media:

Facebook: facebook.com/apostlegeter

Twitter: @apostlegeter

Instagram: @apostlegeter

LinkedIn: linkedin.com/in/apostlegeter

www.darriusgeter.com

www.ingramcontent.com/pod-product-compliance
Lightning Source LLC
Chambersburg PA
CBHW051213290426
44109CB00021B/2435